THE R
of Jesus & Mary

JOYFUL LUMINOUS SORROWFUL GLORIOUS

M. Jean Frisk, S.T.L.

Pauline
BOOKS & MEDIA
Boston

Library of Congress Cataloging in Publication Data

Frisk, M. Jean.
  The Rosary of Jesus and Mary : mysteries for Christian prayer /
M. Jean Frisk.
      p. cm.
Includes bibliographical references.
  ISBN 0-8198-6477-3
  1. Mysteries of the Rosary. I. Title.
  BT303.F75 2003
  242'.74—dc21

                                                    2003001595

Cover Art: Bro. Anthony-Joseph Dusza, Little Brothers of St. Francis

Printed and published in the U.S.A. by Pauline Books & Media, 50 Saint Pauls Avenue, Boston, MA 02130-3491.

www.pauline.org

Pauline Books & Media is the publishing house of the Daughters of St. Paul, an international congregation of women religious serving the Church with the communications media.

1 2 3 4 5 6 7 8 9   11 10 09 08 07 06 05 04 03

*For João Pozzobon, Mary Jessica,
and all who lovingly spread the Gospel
through the Rosary*

CONTENTS

Preface

The Rosary is like a journey that begins and ends at home. This journey encompasses the story of Jesus on earth. With every human life, the beginning is not with ourselves alone, but with others who have in some way said yes to our existence.

Jesus Christ comes to us from the Father, and full circle—though he never leaves us—he returns to the Father. Nevertheless, the Savior chose to come among us like every human life—with the consent and in the womb of a woman, the virgin named Mary. He desired his human beginning and every aspect of his life on earth to be freely accepted with a decision to be associated with him, or, sadly, to be rejected. Jesus obliges no one to love him. Such is true love.

To pray the Rosary means to look at Jesus through Mary's eyes, through Mary's heart, for none can be found who loved him more faithfully. She journeys with him from the moment of his conception, through his death, resurrection, and ascension until she one day joins him in that eternal home called heaven.

Mary wonders, she questions, she reflects, she responds. Mary is there for Jesus, but also for others. Nothing shakes her faithful, loving commitment. Nothing deadens her prayer or hinders her service. She who is his first human teacher, learns from him to master life. She becomes his mirror, and where she walks, his blessings flow. Love wells forth everywhere, wherever this story is told.

So it is that the Rosary is the "epitome of the whole Gospel,"[1] and Mary herself is a "compendium of the entire Gospel"[2] and "a living catechism."[3] All who are baptized in Christ are called to live and love like Mary, who teaches us like no other what faithful discipleship means.

For that is our task: When we take the Rosary in hand and let the beads slip through our fingers, we walk full circle with Mary as our loving teacher, who will contemplate the face of her beloved and divine Son with us until our lives, too, like hers, will mirror Christ's being and actions here on earth.

---

1. *Catechism of the Catholic Church,* n. 971.

2. Pope Pius XII (papacy: 1939–1958), *Acta Apostolicæ Sedis* (AAS) 38 (1946), 419.

3. *Catechesi Tradendæ,* Pope John Paul II, AAS 71-10-16 (1979), 1278–1340.

THE JOYFUL MYSTERIES

*To meditate upon the "joyful" mysteries...
is to enter into the ultimate causes and the
deepest meaning of Christian joy. It is to
focus on the realism of the mystery of the
Incarnation and on the obscure foreshad-
owing of the mystery of the saving passion.
Mary leads us to discover the secret of Christian joy, reminding us that Christianity is,
first and foremost,* euangelion, *"good news,"
which has as its heart and its whole content
the person of Jesus Christ, the Word made
flesh, the one Savior of the world.*

(On the Most Holy Rosary, n. 20)[4]

---

4. Pope John Paul II, Apostolic Letter, *Rosarium Virginis Mariæ*
(October 16, 2002), Pauline Books & Media, Boston.

THE ANNUNCIATION

Who would know of Mary today were it not for the call she received and her thoughtful response? God the Triune called her, not face to face in the tremendous power of divine majesty, but through a messenger given the name Gabriel.

Gabriel singles out this Mary from all other Marys by greeting her as the favored one. He bids her to rejoice! The Lord is with her (cf. Lk 1:28). Mary wonders. The Scriptures tell us she is *perplexed* (cf. Lk 1:29) and needs to think over what this meant. She is not to be afraid. God esteems and blesses her. She is to be the first earthly dwelling of this God, knit in the warmth of her womb. He who is and has been with her since her own beginning now wishes to be so united with her, flesh in flesh, that they are one in this initial part of the Son's human journey. Her question is not a *why* but a *how*.

When Mary is assured that her God, "the Most High," directs all things according to a loving plan, she freely consents to his loving call. "Here am I, the servant of the Lord; let it be with me according to your word" (Lk 1:38).

If it is the Father's plan to unite all things in Christ (cf. Eph 1:10), then the whole of the universe is in some way touched by the divine favor with which the Father looks upon Mary and makes her the Mother of his Son. The whole of humanity, in turn, is embraced by the *fiat* with which she readily agrees to the will of God *(On the Most Holy Rosary,* n. 20).

Eternal Father, Father of us all, and my Father, what are the messages you will send my way today, tomorrow, a year from now? How will you call me and remind me to seek your loving plan—for surely you will do so! Will I be open to your call and seek your face in each greeting? Will I, like Mary, rely on your power, on your overshadowing love, and journey one more day homeward as your servant? Father, allow Christ Jesus to dwell in me and in those I love! Let it be with us according to your word.

The Visitation

Gabriel consoles Mary with wonderful news. Her cousin Elizabeth "in her old age has also conceived a son" (Lk 1:36). The infinite Most High could have used any other means to prove that with God, nothing is impossible. God chooses a human thing, and makes fruitful a relationship between two who are faithful to God's service and to one another. The young Mary rejoices and hurries to share the older couple's joy.

Does Mary sense the new life within her as she journeys toward Elizabeth? Can she dialogue with the God of life interwoven with her very being? Does she travel alone or is Joseph with her sharing the unspoken joy of God's presence among them? What we do not know we may imagine for ourselves in prayerful wonder.

We do know what Scripture tells us of the miracle of the greeting, the encounter of these two child-bearing women: Mary, the Christ-bearer; Elizabeth, bearer of John who will announce the coming of the Lamb of God. Baby John leaps for joy in his mother's womb. Elizabeth knows as only a mother knows and she blesses Mary again and again. Elizabeth is filled with faith and knows that Mary is blessed, "she who believed that there would be a fulfillment of what was spoken to her by the Lord" (Lk 1:45).

Mary joins the inheritance of her ancestors and sings her praise of God like Hannah and others before her. Her *Magnificat* is a song that continues to be sung by the Church in every age.

Mary, let me join you in prayer. As real as my fingers touch these beads, may my spirit, too, know the reality of God with us as you did. I take the sacred text in hand—and sacred I believe it is. I turn to Luke 1:46-58. Ancient traditions tell me these infancy narratives are written from your point of view, the memory of how you prayed. Could it have been that the Child Jesus learned to pray so warmly and tenderly to his Father from you? Teach me, too, Mary!

May I rejoice in God my Savior and magnify his holy name. May I know our gracious God as the Mighty One who does great things for me and all those dear to me. May I remember his mercy and faithful love at all times and everywhere. May I become for him a God-bearer as you were, by his goodness and power filled with grace, the grace of my baptismal commitment made fruitful. Wherever I walk, may his loving kindness touch others through me as it did through you.

Jesus, Mary's firstborn Son,
dwells among us

THE NATIVITY

"And she gave birth to her firstborn son and wrapped him in bands of cloth, and laid him in a manger" (Lk 2:7). Perhaps no story is told so often or illustrated so richly as the birth of Jesus. There is an abundance of active players in this marvelous drama of the Word who became flesh and lived among us. "And we have seen his glory, the glory as of a father's only son, full of grace and truth" (Jn 1:14). Angels and shepherds, Joseph and Mary, innkeepers and kings, legends and reality, winters turn summer, cold hearts turn generous —hunger everywhere to be touched by the love of the little child in the stable.

Mary and Joseph watched the riot of tender homage and love unfold, and all who heard the joyous good news were amazed, for it was proclaimed that the Messiah was born. So down the centuries, little drummers and Christmas roses, holly and huckleberry, pheasant and pie, people and priests—everyone and everything is transformed in the great dance of the Incarnation, when divinity takes on humanity and humanity learns to celebrate as never before.

Swiftly will these joyous days turn to flight, to exile, and to the grief of innocents, but for the nativity's holy night and dawning day, there can only be immeasurable gratitude and joy.

Mary, you treasured all these words and pondered them in your heart. Your memory of these events echoes in my heart as I in turn try to ponder and pray. In all the Savior's human needs for food, clothing, and care, you were there—joyfully, gladly, faithfully, with a love full to bursting. In our mutual prayer and in the work I am called to do, let the Savior be born anew every day in heart after heart.

Jesus is presented in the temple

THE PRESENTATION

"As it is written in the law of the Lord, 'Every first-born male shall be designated as holy to the Lord'" (Lk 2:23). And so Joseph and Mary bring Jesus to Jerusalem to present him in the temple to God. They meet Simeon, "a man righteous and devout" (Lk 2:25) and Anna, a prophet who "worshiped there with fasting and prayer night and day" (Lk 2:36–37). Those holy ones, man and woman, recognize the "light for revelation to the Gentiles" and for glory to God's people Israel (Lk 2:32).

The story of the presentation in the temple manifests the glory and destiny of the Savior—a sign of contradiction, "A sign that will be opposed so that the inner thoughts of many will be revealed" (Lk 2:34–35). At the same time, Simeon tells Mary that her soul will be pierced by a sword. Her life will ever be interwoven with the destiny of her Son. Her mother's heart will watch in joy when he is praised and stand in sorrow when he is opposed, but she will remain the servant of the sacrifice, unconditionally adoring the Father's will for her beloved Son.

Every woman of Israel might dream of giving birth to the savior who would set his people free from op-

8

pression and poverty. Did Mary ever imagine it would be her? Or, as ancient legends tell us, did she desire only to serve the elected one? In the temple she heard the prophecies fulfilled. She is the mother of the child to whom "all were looking for the redemption of Jerusalem" (Lk 2:36).

Mary, ancient tradition says you were brought to the temple where you spent your childhood learning the history, prophecies, and prayers of your people. If it is so, and our Church celebrates it so, did you recognize Anna and she you? Was Anna surprised it was you who would be the Christ-bearer? Or did she perhaps suspect that you were indeed the beloved and favored one of God—from joyful child to young mother? Mary, as favored, loved, and happy as you were to be chosen and to hold this child so intimately close as your very own, life's paths nevertheless hid a sword for you at every bend. In my hands I hold a wreath of roses. Midst all the joy, there will ever be thorns, little pricks to pierce reality. Teach me, Mary, to see the Father's love behind every sword that pierces my heart and the hearts of my loved ones.

THE FINDING IN THE TEMPLE

Luke tells us that Joseph and Mary went to Jerusalem every year for the Passover festival. Time and again they return to the temple to worship and to celebrate the traditions of their people. The passing over of the Jewish nation into freedom centuries before remained a sign of hope for the freedom yet to come. Joy and celebration is only possible where gratitude abounds.

But the twelve-year-old Jesus celebrates in his own way. He is growing, becoming strong, and being filled with wisdom. The favor of God is upon him (cf. Lk 2:40). He insists on knowing more, searching deeper; he must do everything to understand. Above all, he is at home in the temple, his Father's house (cf. Lk 2:49).

Time escaped, the days passed. Jesus knew the Father and recognized what belonged to the Father. The very first words recorded in the Scriptures from Jesus himself tell us who he is: the Son of the Father. The Father's name spoken by Jesus will be recorded 166 times in the Gospels. Jesus says to his anxious parents who have sought for him three days: "Why were you searching for me? Did you not know that I must be in my Father's house?" (Lk 2:49) Scholars tell us that the

Scripture passage could also mean Jesus was compelled to be "(involved) in my Father's affairs" or "among those belonging to my Father."[5]

But Joseph and Mary did not understand what Jesus meant or where his journey would lead—that he would be the new Passover Lamb for the freedom of all peoples.

Mary, what did you think when you saw your child sitting among the teachers? According to the sacred text, you didn't expect to find him there. And what did it do to your heart to hear your beloved Son speak to you as if what he did shouldn't matter to you? There could be no answers yet, but you "treasured all these things" in your heart (Lk 2:51). Mary, when my loved ones and I lose our orientation on the Lord and cannot find or understand him, please help us to continue seeking him and to be amazed at the Father's wise plan for our lives.

---

5. *New Jerome Biblical Commentary,* 43:36, p. 684.

THE MYSTERIES OF LIGHT

In these mysteries, apart from the miracle of Cana, the presence of Mary remains in the background. *The Gospels make only the briefest reference to her occasional presence at one moment or other during the preaching of Jesus (cf. Mk 3:31–35; Jn 2:12), and they give no indication that she was present at the Last Supper and the institution of the Eucharist. Yet the role she assumed at Cana in some way accompanies Christ throughout his ministry. The revelation made directly by the Father at the Baptism in the Jordan and echoed by John the Baptist is*

placed upon Mary's lips at Cana, and it be-
comes the great maternal counsel which
Mary addresses to the Church of every age:
"Do whatever he tells you" (Jn 2:5). This
counsel is a fitting introduction to the
words and signs of Christ's public ministry,
and it forms the Marian foundation of all
the "mysteries of light."

(On the Most Holy Rosary, n. 21)

THE BAPTISM OF THE LORD

All four Gospels tell the story of the opening of the heavens and the Spirit descending on Jesus before he is about to begin his public ministry. The event takes place when Jesus comes to the Jordan River where his cousin John is baptizing those who accept his call to repent and prepare the way for the one who is to come. Jesus leaves behind his hidden life and asks for the baptism, and John agrees, although he knows Jesus is not in need of repentance and transformation. Jesus shows that he is now ready to come, to submit, and to serve the will of the Father.

The Baptizer calls out, "Here is the Lamb of God who takes away the sin of the world!" (Jn 1:29) When the waters have cleansed, the heavens open and the Spirit descends upon Jesus in the form of a dove. Pope John Paul II writes of this moment:

> Here, as Christ descends into the waters, the innocent one who became "sin" for our sake (cf. 2 Cor 5:21), the heavens open wide and the voice of the Father declares him the beloved Son (cf. Mt 3:17 and parallels), while the Spirit descends on him to invest him with the mis-

sion which he is to carry out (*On the Most Holy Rosary,* n. 21).

Does the sacred text tell us Jesus experienced this revelation privately? Or is it a public event filled with radiant light? Does it matter now? It is given to us in the Scriptures as a revelation of Father, Son, and Spirit about to pour out abundant love upon the world where the beloved Son will walk among the people, along the by-ways and through the cities where he will pass.

It is after this testimony of the Father's confirmed love and the overshadowing of the Spirit like a gentle dove that Jesus goes into the desert for forty days before beginning his public ministry.

Mary, what would you have seen if you were at the Jordan? Would you have heard the Father's voice and seen the hovering Spirit? Would you have seen the waters make their rings around your Son, noted his radiance, and been touched by his light as he walked away into the desert? Would you have wanted to follow him?

Slowly he left you, left the hidden life you shared. You watched him grow while he learned the skills of Joseph and bore the burdens of the day. Did he sometimes go away to pray? Was it different as the forty days he was away in the Galilean desert days stretched on? He is your beloved Son and you waited.

Did the Spirit you shared comfort you to know he did the Father's will, and when he returned, was he ready for his hour? Mary, with you he prepared thirty years for the Father's call and the Spirit's sign. Did he come home once more to tell you? In the quiet, as I finger one pearl after another, may I wait with you at the loom to hear his voice at the door?

THE WEDDING AT CANA

Pope John Paul II writes of Cana, "Another mystery of light is the first of the signs, given at Cana (cf. Jn 2:1–12), when Christ changes water into wine and opens the hearts of the disciples to faith, thanks to the intervention of Mary, the first among believers" (*On the Most Holy Rosary,* n. 21).

Think of a Jewish wedding with finery and festivity, music and dance, delicacies and choice wine, kin and friends, laughter and song—everyone generously welcome. "The mother of Jesus was there. Jesus and his disciples had also been invited to the wedding" (Jn 2:1–2). How was it that the wine ran out? Did Jesus bring more friends than the hosts anticipated? Whatever the reason, whatever the symbol of the wine meant to all of them, it was Mary who noticed the new couple's embarrassment and did not want the celebration to end. Did she somehow know it was time for him to establish the Father's kingdom?

Mary speaks seldom in the pages of Sacred Scripture, though her presence is felt as she accompanies her son throughout. All the more will this final record testify to her own committed faith. She knows he is Lord.

She knows he is mercy and goodness. She hears his strange words, "Woman, what concern is that to you and to me? My hour has not come" (Jn 2:4). But she also knows that loving kindness will be his measure over and above all else. Her prayer does not beg or plead, badger or insist. She states the situation and trusts in simple belief that he will solve the need in his own time.

"They have no wine" (Jn 2:3).

"Do whatever he tells you" (Jn 2:5).

His response was a quiet thing. He required that a chore not be neglected. Empty water jars must be filled, and an abundance of the finest vintage resulted at his word. "Jesus did this, the first of his signs, in Cana of Galilee, and revealed his glory, and his disciples believed in him" (Jn 2:11).

Mary, why did Jesus call you "woman" and question your mutual concern? You know precisely that he does care and has the means to do something about it, or you wouldn't have mentioned it. No longer mother charging son with a task, but woman next to man, mutually sharing a service to be given. Is he counting on you in new ways? Are you to share his work in a woman's way?

Mary, teach me to notice things as you did. Make me aware of the failing wine, and urge me to do something about it—not by my own grand schemes, but by his name and power. He will not spare me my share of the load for it is I who must fill the jars, but he who will work the miracle. O Mary, if I could but believe and love as you did even when at first he seems to say no!

Jesus proclaims the kingdom of God
and calls us to conversion

THE PROCLAMATION OF THE KINGDOM

The story of Jesus continues. He returns from the desert where he has been tempted to walk away from his mission. He returns to Galilee "proclaiming the good news of God, and saying, 'The time is fulfilled, and the kingdom of God has come near; repent, and believe in the good news'" (Mk 1:14–15).

The kingdom Jesus preached is both now and to come. Jesus said he "must proclaim the good news of the kingdom of God" for he was sent for this purpose (Lk 4:43), and he sent his twelve out to do the same (Lk 9:2). The prayer Jesus taught us tells us that it is his Father's kingdom he is to establish, not a place, but *the action* of doing the Father's will "on earth as it is in heaven" (Mt 6:10). Over and over, Jesus described the kingdom in parables and stories depicting good and evil actions, which welcome or hinder God's presence among us and will, with God's gracious mercy, bring us home finally to the bosom of the Father as our ultimate destiny.

The kingdom is like good seed sown in hearts, a mustard seed—the tiny word or deed—that mushrooms like a well-watered tree spreading its fruits over the earth, the leaven bringing life to the sodden lump of flour, the pearl precious in the Lord's eyes. Jesus uses symbols, objects, the common and the rare—both are valuable in his eyes—to teach us what delights the Father.

According to the various translations there are 121 Gospel verses that speak of the kingdom—121 times this decade of the Rosary could bring a fresh new thought for those who take the sacred text in hand and search for teachings on the kingdom. From the Beatitudes to the Our Father we learn to master life and to do our part in building up the Father's kingdom. We learn that unless we change and become like children we will never enter the kingdom of heaven. "Whoever becomes humble like this child is the greatest in the kingdom of heaven" (Mt 18:3–5). Perhaps children teach us best how to ask for the gifts of the kingdom, perceiving by nature their dependence on the giver. And Jesus adds, "Whoever welcomes one such child in my name welcomes me" (Mt 13:5).

Mary, did you learn to trust the Father in all your moves from place to place? In your home at Nazareth, did Jesus speak the Father's name: our Father, my Father? And when Jesus preached the kingdom, did he draw on his experience of you and Joseph in the everyday life of the village?

Mary, how beautiful the mountainside where Jesus taught the blessings! Were you among the crowd that listened that day, looking out across the lake and hearing him speak of the happiness of the poor in spirit, of those who mourn, of the meek, those who hunger and thirst for righteousness, the merciful, the pure in heart, the peacemakers, and the persecuted? And did you nod your head in agreement, rejoicing in heart because you had experienced the kingdom in him in your own home?

Mary, while my circle of beads reaches midway, let me sit beside you and listen; then, when all the listening is done, help me live these Beatitudes as you did.

THE TRANSFIGURATION

> The mystery of light *par excellence* is the Transfigura-
> tion, traditionally believed to have taken place on
> Mount Tabor. The glory of the Godhead shines forth
> from the face of Christ as the Father commands the as-
> tonished Apostles to "listen to him" (cf. Lk 9:35 and par-
> allels), and to prepare to experience with him the agony
> of the passion, so as to come with him to the joy of the
> resurrection and a life transfigured by the Holy Spirit
> (*On the Most Holy Rosary,* n. 21).

Jesus repeatedly proclaims the kingdom and its
coming. He works miracles, feeds the multitudes, journeys far and wide, forgives sins, and teaches marvelous
wisdom for daily life. He simply brings joy everywhere.
Hearts are buoyant with expectation of the good times
to come. But shortly before the transfiguration, Jesus begins to tell his disciples, "The Son of Man must undergo
great suffering, and be rejected,…and be killed, and on
the third day be raised" (Lk 9:22). Not only does Jesus
speak of his own destiny, he tells his followers they
must also share his cross by taking up their own (cf. Lk
9:20).

How confusing this must have been! How could the mind grasp it! One moment, Cana's abundance and riotous joy; another, Bethsaida's thousands are fed; storms are calmed, little daughters are restored to life, demons are expelled. Why on earth should this man die!

And Jesus takes a chosen three away to pray. High on a mountainside they experience the Son of God in his transparent glory, a radiance not found on earth. In the face of Jesus, they glimpse the glory to come. They want to stay. No talk here of death or a premonition of pain. "Master, it is good for us to be here; let us make three dwellings, one for you, one for Moses, and one for Elijah" (Lk 9:33). "A cloud came and overshadowed them; and they were terrified as they entered the cloud. Then from the cloud came a voice that said, 'This is my Son, my Chosen; listen to him!'" (Lk 9:34–35)

The command is given: Listen to him! It is time to be silent and wait for him to speak. There is a why to the suffering and there is a fullness of light to follow. They have seen his divinity in his face. They have experienced the Spirit's overshadowing and the Father's voice. Indeed, they will never forget the mountain.

Mary, how many times, during those thirty years of Jesus' life at home with you, did your heart sing: "It is good for us to be here!" Every day in its own small ways could be Tabor, a place of revelation, a place of prayer. For you, did the secret of Tabor consist in doing ordinary things extraordinarily well—because Love was always present, always the reason?

Peter, James, and John were chosen to witness his Godhead and his glory. They would lead his Church, and give all for the kingdom in other ways. They needed the mountain experience for strength in times to come. So many of us do!

But, Mary, for most of us, we must seek his radiant light and the Father's voice like you did—in the sounds of street and village and home, the distant gaze of a young son's search, laughter at stories well told, delight in the daily task well done. Let me spend one day at home with you to learn his glory in little things.

Jesus institutes the Eucharist as the sacramental expression of the Paschal Mystery

THE INSTITUTION OF THE EUCHARIST

"Now before the festival of the Passover, Jesus knew that his hour had come to depart from this world and go to the Father. Having loved his own who were in the world, he loved them to the end" (Jn 13:1). At the end of his journey on earth, Jesus will be forever present in his passion, death, and resurrection. In this ultimate self-giving we call Eucharist, thanksgiving, we find the Jesus who loves.

If we didn't know better, we might think that Jesus was humanly condemned to die because his love just couldn't be real. Had there ever been any lover of the people like this before, and would there ever be again? Jesus came from the Father to reveal the Father's love, and at his last supper on earth he tells us:

> "As the Father has loved me, so I have loved you; abide in my love. If you keep my commandments, you will abide in my love, just as I have kept my Father's commandments and abide in his love. I have said these things to you so that my joy may be in you, and that your joy may be complete.

> "This is my commandment, that you love one another as I have loved you. No one has greater love than this, to lay down one's life for one's friends. You are my friends if you do what I command you" (Jn 15:9–14).

Perhaps we want to turn in sorrow to Jesus and ask him: How is it possible to love one another once the raw reality and summation of our moral and physical weaknesses come to light for what they really are? Do sinners believe they are worthy of love? Do the arrogant believe anyone is worthy of their love? Could that be one of the secrets of the Eucharist? When we eat this bread and drink this cup, it is Jesus who establishes his presence in us. When we look into the face of the other, we see there the beloved face of Christ who unites us all in his body—the face of Christ serving, loving, laughing, weeping, suffering, dying, and rising.

The Eucharist is a sign of unity, a bond of charity—the greatest possible prayer ascending to the Father, the "place" of the Spirit's overshadowing like no other. Together we consume the loving Christ, real and present, who is to nourish us and act in us. Like Mary, who was the first to bear him in her body, we too may take him into our body and become, like her, a Christ-bearer for our world.

Mary, were you in the upper room when the bread was broken and the cup blessed? Did you help prepare the unleavened bread and the little lamb?

Were you watching and listening, taking in and un-derstanding the long farewell discourse, and was it familiar to you when your Son spoke of the Father's love and their oneness? Did you share the broken bread and the cup of wine that first night—and re-member when he dwelt within your womb? You above all would know what it meant for the Christ to dwell within.

Did you see Judas leave and worry about the look on his face? What premonitions were in your mother's heart, and could you ask the Father to strengthen Jesus when he went away to the garden to pray?

Mary, in the quiet now, when all have left the banquet, let me help you clear the table and gather the fragments—wondering, loving, adoring. Help me, Mary, to find my place at the communion table of his Church and give ceaseless, quiet thanks.

THE SORROWFUL MYSTERIES

Behold the man!

Ecce homo: the meaning, origin and fulfillment of man is to be found in Christ, the God who humbles himself out of love "even unto death, death on a cross" (Phil 2:8). The sorrowful mysteries help the believer to relive the death of Jesus, to stand at the foot of the cross beside Mary, to enter with her into the depths of God's love for man and to experience all its life-giving power.

(On the Most Holy Rosary, n. 22)

Jesus suffers agony in the garden of Gethsemane

THE AGONY IN THE GARDEN

The hour Jesus speaks about has come. He will return to the Father. He will go the way before us and make it possible for us one day to be with the God he has revealed as *Abba*. It is amazing to read the seventeenth chapter of John's Gospel. Jesus prays for us at the Paschal meal with a gentle strength and intimacy that must have stopped the very breath of those gathered with him.

> "Father, the hour has come; glorify your Son so that the Son may glorify you, since you have given him authority over all people, to give eternal life to all whom you have given him. And this is eternal life, that they may know you, the only true God, and Jesus Christ whom you have sent. I glorified you on earth by finishing the work that you gave me to do" (Jn 17:1-5).

> "I have made your name known to those you gave me from the world.... Holy Father, protect them in your name that you have given me, so that they may be one, as we are one" (Jn 17:6, 11).

"Holy Father, protect them in your name...." These sorrowful mysteries are, as Pope John Paul II expresses in his letter, *On the Most Holy Rosary*, "*the culmination of the revelation of God's love* and the source of our salvation" (n. 22). He continues:

> The sequence of meditations begins with Gethsemane, where Christ experiences a moment of great anguish before the will of the Father, against which the weakness of the flesh would be tempted to rebel. There Jesus encounters all the temptations and confronts all the sins of humanity, in order to say to the Father: "Not my will but yours be done" (Lk 22:42 and parallels). This "Yes" of Christ reverses the "No" of our first parents in the Garden of Eden.

Lord Jesus, with the heart of Mary, who was not with you in the garden, let me ask Peter, James, and John to tell me how it was there, for they were with you. She must have questioned—like a mother who wishes to hear the unfolding of every agonizing detail. Like her, I want each facet carved into my heart. They tell me of your anguish and agitation when you asked them to keep awake and pray. Three times you came and asked them to be with you in prayer and vigilance. Three times they nodded away the hour, for they were safe and content with you and the extraordinary things you did.

They have just celebrated communion with you, have been fed the lamb, the bitter herbs, and the fine wine of the Passover meal. And though they

noted your prayer and your anguish, they remem-
bered Tabor—everything had worked out well so far.
No, they did not sense fear or danger. Somehow,
Lord, in spite of your agony, they rested peacefully.
Your mother must have understood. Perhaps she felt
the same way on the flight to Egypt. What you suf-
fered here you suffered alone.

I, too, do not know what to say to you when my
eyes are heavy and I cannot pray, when something
blocks my capacity to share an hour with those who
ask for my prayer. I want to! Truly, I long to be able
to stay awake and watch with you. Like Peter, James,
and John, I promised to be there for you. Forgive me,
Lord! And when I myself suffer the agony of sorrow,
sin, and despair, let me join you in the garden
where drops of your blood remind me that the Fa-
ther waits for my return.

THE SCOURGING AT THE PILLAR

The Rosary beads slipping through my fingers are harmless things, but what if they were bits of bone or metal with spiked edges and were to prick my fingers? Would I continue to let them slip by? The slightest discomfort can distract us from prayer.

The betrayal and trial of Jesus are the background of this mystery. Jesus is dragged from court to court. Finally, he is led before the people. They are given a choice: they can have Barabbas or Jesus. Strange that the name Barabbas means "son of the father." Strange, too, that Pilate gives Jesus a new name, "the king of the Jews" (Jn 18:39). Pilate speaks:

> "Indeed, he has done nothing to deserve death. I will therefore have him flogged and release him." Then they all shouted out together, "Away with this fellow! Release Barabbas for us!" (This was a man who had been put in prison for an insurrection that had taken place in the city, and for murder.) Pilate, wanting to release Jesus, addressed them again; but they kept shouting, "Crucify, crucify him!" (Lk 23:15–21)

Were Mary and the Magdalene struggling in the crowd? What irony to hear the name Barabbas equated with the Son who has come to reveal the loving Abba and his kingdom. What terror must have struck their hearts to hear the crowd scream for Barabbas and to see Jesus led away to be flogged!

Many shrines of Europe contain marble pillars half a man's height. The pillars have iron rings fixed near the top of the stone. We shudder and remember what man can do to man—what human beings can do even to God! Persons so chained would have to bend over the stone exposing their backs to a maximum tautness—until the pain of the leather whip imbedded with bone or metal crushed them to their knees. The flogging was meant to precede crucifixion, to weaken the body and shorten the agony on the cross.

Jesus endured this—every stroke a frenzy against fear, a rage against love. Crush the one who speaks of a peaceful kingdom and a glory not found in this world (cf. Jn 18:36).

Where were you, Mary? Could you hear the lashing and the mockery beyond the courtyard crowd? Could you hear his voice when he spoke to Pilate?

How I wish to hear him speak those words for us today once more! I want the generations to hear him. Just as you did, Mary, I want to write his words indelibly in my heart so that they form my way of viewing all things. "You say that I am a king. For this I was born, and for this I came into the world, to testify to the truth. Everyone who belongs to the truth listens to my voice" (Jn 18:37).

I ask with Pilate, "What is truth?" (Jn 18:38) But I ask it in helplessness before the thousands of issues and images invading my senses each day. Like you, Mary, may I never stop listening. May I never walk away from the Lord in my search for the truth only God can give.

Mary, it sickens me when the splendid scarlet cloak is laid on Jesus' shoulders, hiding his ripped flesh—wounds that continue to bleed in every age. Help me see his enduring love, which alone can lead to truth.

THE CROWNING WITH THORNS

Then the soldiers of the governor took Jesus into the governor's headquarters, and they gathered the whole cohort around him. They stripped him and put a scarlet robe on him, and after twisting some thorns into a crown, they put it on his head. They put a reed in his right hand and knelt before him and mocked him, saying, "Hail, King of the Jews!" They spat on him, and took the reed and struck him on the head. After mocking him, they stripped him of the robe and put his own clothes on him. Then they led him away to crucify him (Mt 27:27–31).

The text tells us that "they" twisted thorns into a crown and put it on his head. Somewhere a commentator on the Shroud of Turin describes the gashes on the head of the man wrapped in it, like a covering pressed into the whole skull. Other writers speak of the thorns near Jerusalem as large and as hard as spike nails. We are caught up in the grotesque physical horror. All the more gruesome when the crowd responds like wolves at the smell of blood: "They kept coming up to him, saying, 'Hail, King of the Jews!' and striking him on the face. Pilate went out again and said to them, 'Look, I am bringing him out to you to let you know that I find no case against him.' …When the chief priests and the police saw him, they shouted, 'Crucify him! Crucify him!'" (Jn 19:3-4, 6)

Artists through the ages have sketched the *Ecce homo*, the face of Christ torn and mutilated that Pilate presents to the people. The artist Roxolana Luchakowski Armstrong has painted beautiful watercolors of the sorrowful mysteries.[6] She portrays the suffering Savior in the foreground of each mystery, while his mother watches in her own inner agony. For the third mystery, Mary grasps the prison bars of a window and peers through, eyes wide with pain as she gazes at his back.

What is it that drives some human beings to howl for blood and death in order to be rid of life's burdens? Why are some driven by viciousness, caught up in the mindless crowd clouded by anger and hate they cannot define? We are free to choose. That is the mystery. Jesus desires to shatter this arrogance once and for all, but not at the cost of human freedom. Indeed, love is not a fluctuating emotion turning with the tide, a coin whose other side is hate. Love is an act of the will set firmly and freely. It is truly up to us to make the choice.

Jesus, your face! How I long to see your face! Yet I cannot deal well with the thorns that tear your face

---

6. These are on display at the Marian Library, International Marian Research Institute in Dayton, Ohio.

*into rivers of blood. But is the horror of your suffer-
ing and every suffering erased simply because I do
not want to see it?*

*Strange! I think of the soldiers' hands that wove
your crown of thorns. Surely their hands were torn
on the thorns, inflicting pain on themselves as they
hurt you. What did they think later while their own
hands slowly healed? Did they feel remorse for the
agony they caused, like I do when my thoughts
lash out uncontrolled? I hope so, Lord, how I hope
so! And did you forgive them even then? I ask you,
Lord: accept my sorrow for the part I play in plaiting
the thorns.*

THE CARRYING OF THE CROSS

John's Gospel makes a point of telling us: "So they took Jesus; and carrying the cross by himself, he went out to what is called The Place of the Skull, which in Hebrew is called Golgotha" (Jn 19:16–17). He and he alone is the Redeemer. Nevertheless, the Gospels of Mark, Matthew, and Luke include Simon of Cyrene who was arbitrarily seized and pressed into service to carry the cross. We must find our way to participate.

It is Luke, writer of the stories of Jesus' infancy, who tells most about the carrying of the cross:

> As they led him away, they seized a man, Simon of Cyrene, who was coming from the country, and they laid the cross on him, and made him carry it behind Jesus. A great number of the people followed him, and among them were women who were beating their breasts and wailing for him. But Jesus turned to them and said, "Daughters of Jerusalem, do not weep for me, but weep for yourselves and for your children. For the days are surely coming when they will say, 'Blessed are the barren, and the wombs that never bore, and the breasts that never nursed.' Then they will begin to say to the mountains, 'Fall on us'; and to the hills, 'Cover us.' For

if they do this when the wood is green, what will happen when it is dry?" (Lk 23:26–31)

For centuries pilgrims have traveled to Jerusalem to walk the path that Jesus took on his way to Golgotha. They read these passages, and some take up the crossbeam like Simon in symbolic imitation. The earliest traditions say the practice began with Mary, mother of Jesus, who would walk the path each day. A sixth-century manuscript includes these passages:

> In the year 345 (of the Seleucian era, i.e., A.D. 34), in the month of the latter Teshrin, my Lady Mary came forth from her house and went to the tomb of the Messiah, because day by day she used to go and weep there.... And the watchmen came in and said to the priests, "Mary comes in the evening and in the morning, and prays there." And there was a commotion in Jerusalem concerning my Lady Mary; and the priests went to the judge and said to him, "My Lord, send and order Mary not to go and pray at the grave and Golgotha."[7]

Mary, where were you in the crowd? Did you see Simon and the wailing women? The legends are many. There is the story that you waited at the cor-

---

7. Way of the Cross: "The Departure of my Lady Mary from this world," translated from the Syriac by Dr. William Wright, Journal of Sacred Literature, April 1865. (This account is copied from a 6th century manuscript.) For a fuller account of the traditions associated with Mary's place in the Stations of the Cross, see: www.udayton.edu/mary, then use the search engine.

ner by your mother's house—he would know, you would know. To the Roman soldiers you were just another woman in the crowd. But it is not so. You walked with him to the summit, joined inseparably with him and his destiny, associated like Eve to Adam for the new covenant, cooperating fully in redemption.

A prisoner of the Dachau concentration camp wrote lines of poetry to describe your meeting:

An ocean of sorrow wells in both hearts,
but nothing can reverse their decision
to resolutely accept the Father's will
and go the way of suffering together.[8]

Mary, where am I in the great number of people following you that day, or do I only imagine that I could have the strength to walk the hill and share the sorrow? Would I, instead, have hid? Give me your courage to journey with you, like you, faithfully.

---

8. Prisoner of Dachau: Father Joseph Kentenich, Founder of the Schoenstatt Movement as published in *Heavenwards,* American edition, Jonathan Niehaus, trans., 1992.

THE CRUCIFIXION

"Many women were also there, looking on from a distance; they had followed Jesus from Galilee and had provided for him" (Mt 27:55).

> Meanwhile, standing near the cross of Jesus were his mother, and his mother's sister, Mary the wife of Clopas, and Mary Magdalene. When Jesus saw his mother and the disciple whom he loved standing beside her, he said to his mother, "Woman, here is your son." Then he said to the disciple, "Here is your mother." And from that hour the disciple took her into his own home (Jn 19:25-27).

As the Holy Father's letter tells it, "The Lord is cast into the most abject suffering: *Ecce homo*! This abject suffering reveals not only the love of God but also the meaning of man himself" (*On the Most Holy Rosary,* n. 22). In all the Gospel narratives concerning the crucifixion, powerful and noble men interact in the condemnation and torture of Jesus. What they say and how they act is beyond all natural human instincts, which preserve life and fight for freedom. Is it their blinded brokenness which mistakes Jesus' acts of love and mercy for a desire to control others with manipulative power? Are they afraid that Jesus will unseat their own secure—

or insecure—positions? In the face of such error, who can arbitrate? The crucifixion is the epitome of injustice, and Jesus himself permits it.

To whom should I address my prayer?

Or should I pray at all?

It is the vast, empty time, the dying—"For everything there is a season, and a time for every matter under heaven: a time to be born, and a time to die; a time to plant, and a time to pluck up what is planted; a time to kill, and a time to heal,…time to keep silence, and a time to speak" (Eccl 3:1–4, 7).

It is time now to wonder about death and my meaning as the beads slip by. I wait with John and the many women; I wait with the one woman whose pain is more intense than birthing. But then, it is indeed a new birth she shares. We wait in the dying for the bonds of death to break. Silence is best here.

But the silence is only within my soul as I wait and don't know how to pray. Around me soldiers quarrel over dice, the earth shakes and rocks split, the great curtain of the sanctuary is torn in two, there is wailing, wailing and dread—noise upon noise, confusion everywhere, and evil, but not here where Mary quietly stands, and, beside her, John. I watch him, the Lord's beloved, but he too is silent in the waiting.

The Lamb speaks now and then. I strain to hear and to remember, but it is the blood and water flowing from his precious side that holds me as I miss the moment of his dying. I want to put my hand there, as later Thomas will, to touch the living substance and let it wash over me. So fragrant the sacrifice; so precious the opening of his heart.

If only I could go within and stay forever, like Mary does, silently nested in the great welcoming womb of his heart!

THE GLORIOUS MYSTERIES

The contemplation of Christ's face cannot stop at the image of the Crucified One. He is the Risen One!

(*John Paul II,* Novo Millennio Ineunte, *n. 28*)

The Rosary has always expressed this knowledge born of faith and invited the believer to pass beyond the darkness of the passion in order to gaze upon Christ's glory in the resurrection and ascension…. The glorious mysteries thus lead the faithful to greater hope for the eschatological goal toward which they journey as members of the

pilgrim People of God in history. This can only impel them to bear courageous witness to that "good news" which gives meaning to their entire existence.

(On the Most Holy Rosary, n. 23)

THE RESURRECTION

> Contemplating the Risen One, Christians *rediscover the reasons for their own faith* (cf. 1 Cor 15:14) and relive the joy not only of those to whom Christ appeared—the Apostles, Mary Magdalene, and the disciples on the road to Emmaus—but also *the joy of Mary,* who must have had an equally intense experience of the new life of her glorified Son (*On the Most Holy Rosary,* n. 22).

The extraordinary birth and strange events, the miracles and messages, the unjust death, the words—all of them—would have no meaning without the resurrection of Jesus. In hindsight, his followers remembered he said it would happen. But it took a while for the memory to register. Faith needed nurturing. Meanwhile, stones roll away, women tell their amazing tales, men run to an empty tomb and go home again, a shroud lies rumpled on the floor, a face cloth is rolled up in a separate place. Could it be? Is the incredible true? He is risen!

But things are not the same. Jesus does not return to his little band to journey with them day in and day out from village to village. He goes where he will, alone, and meets those whose hearts are open to recognize him. Even his voice needs its time for recognition. "Were not our hearts burning within us…while he was opening the Scriptures to us?" (Lk 35:32) It is in the breaking of the bread that they finally recognize him (cf. Lk 24:35).

Now and in every age there are women carrying spices, men journeying to Emmaus, fish breakfasts on the shore, Magdalenes weeping in the garden, Thomases doubting and tenderly loving, disciples believing, Peters repenting, and Judases despairing. But he is risen and it all makes sense—or will—in his time and place.

Where were you, Mary, on Easter morning? And why are the Scriptures silent? Some saints say Jesus came first to you—an encounter so private it remains hidden like the thirty years you spent with him in Bethlehem, Egypt, Nazareth, Jerusalem, and Cana. So little is publicly known.

So, did he come as I would hope a son of mine would? Did he allow you to take his scarred hands and feel the resurrected glory in the still fresh wounds? Did he need a new garment woven by your tenderness? Or had angels made one to replace the one he left behind? You smile, I smile. It's a secret you'll both keep.

Or, Mary, did you whisper the Father's name together in awesome reverence, recounting his won-

drous deeds and marvelous plan? Or was it enough for you to know at Magdalene's word: He lives, Mary, he lives! So shall you, and so shall I—forever.

THE ASCENSION

Biblical scholars tell us that the resurrection includes the ascension. Jesus' body has truly risen. He does human things—walking, talking, touching, eating—and yet his transfigured body is not limited to time and space, but it is also free now in new ways. "Christ's humanity can no longer be confined to earth and belongs henceforth only to the Father's divine realm" (*Catechism of the Catholic Church*, n. 645).

He told us, "I came from the Father and have come into the world; again, I am leaving the world and am going to the Father" (Jn 16:28). There comes a moment when Jesus finally ascends to take his throne forty days after defeating death. He will come one more time, as recorded in the sacred text, to Paul (1 Cor 15:3-8), but today Jesus returns to the Father.

> Henceforth Christ is *seated at the right hand of the Father:* "By 'the Father's right hand' we understand the glory and honor of divinity, where he who exists as Son of God before all ages, indeed as God, of one being with the Father, is seated bodily after he became incarnate and his flesh was glorified" *(CCC,* n. 663).

Being seated at the Father's right hand signifies the inauguration of the Messiah's kingdom, the fulfillment of the prophet Daniel's vision concerning the Son of man: "To him was given dominion and glory and kingdom, that all peoples, nations, and languages should serve him; his dominion is an everlasting dominion, which shall not pass away, and his kingdom one that shall not be destroyed." After this event the apostles became witnesses of the "kingdom [that] will have no end" *(CCC,* n. 664).

As our beads slip by, perhaps we are baffled by the immensity of it all. He is risen and with us, but also far from us on the throne of heaven—close and distant, near and far.

Mary, can you make the immensity manageable? How can I relate to him now? It was so easy when he sat by the well and walked through wheat fields. Like a child, may I ask a thousand questions? The disciples on the way to Emmaus returned to Jerusalem and "found the eleven and their companions gathered together" (Lk 24:33). Were you and the women among them? I know you were there when they returned from the ascension (cf. Acts 1:14), but were you there when Jesus stood among them, calming their fears and doubts, wishing them peace? Did you listen as he "opened their minds to understand the scriptures" (Lk 24:45)?

Was it like the old days with all the warmth and joy of his presence, when the Marys and Marthas sat at his feet and served him and the men jostled to be on his right and left? Was there laughter again and singing? And when he led them as far as Bethany (cf. Lk 24:50) did you go along? Was there one more stop at Lazarus' beloved home? Was it the same as before in the sunshine of his human divine love, yet different, too? For all of you know this is the last time—he is going where he has promised. So perhaps the laughter has its own rich melancholy, like all farewells among those who love one another.

You and they cannot go with him—yet! But here on the mount where the olives grow, the mourning and weeping are done. The questions don't all need answers, for it is enough to be enfolded in his blessing now and worship him (cf. Lk 24:50).

Mary, what were your thoughts at the setting of the sun on that ascension day? Were you, like the others, filled with joy upon returning to Jerusalem (cf. Lk 24:50)? Let me walk with you in the evening of the day and wait with you for him at dawn—certain he will return.

The Holy Spirit descends upon the early Church

THE DESCENT OF THE HOLY SPIRIT

At the center of this unfolding sequence of the glory of the Son and the Mother, the Rosary sets before us the third glorious mystery, Pentecost, which reveals the face of the Church as a family gathered together with Mary, enlivened by the powerful outpouring of the Spirit and ready for the mission of evangelization. The contemplation of this scene, like that of the other glorious mysteries, ought to lead the faithful to an ever greater appreciation of their new life in Christ, lived in the heart of the Church, a life of which the scene of Pentecost itself is the great "icon" (*On the Most Holy Rosary*, n. 23).

Each year, fifty days after the resurrection of Jesus, we celebrate the wonderful thing that happened to the first Christian community. "They were all together in one place" (Acts 2:1) as was their custom after the ascension of Jesus when he told them to return to Jerusalem and wait until they had been "clothed with power from on high" (Lk 24:49).

The apostles were there, "constantly devoting themselves to prayer, together with certain women, including Mary the mother of Jesus, as well as his brothers" (Acts

1:14). About 120 gathered together whom Peter called friends (Acts 1:15).

Peter has taken initiative and begun to organize the situation now that Jesus is gone. Matthias is chosen to take Judas' place, for the Lord had appointed twelve to bear leadership among the believers. All is ready for the Lord's work to continue, "that repentance and forgiveness of sins...be proclaimed in his name to all nations beginning from Jerusalem" (Lk 24:47). They were witnesses of these things, and Jesus promised to send his Spirit to teach them how to fulfill their mission.

But fifty days alone, waiting, without the Lord.... How should life go on?

Pentecost, Mary! Another festival of your people, a pilgrimage festival, they say. Did you look forward to the holiday and prepare for it in the usual way? But he wasn't there, nor would he be. Did you miss him so, miss mixing his favorite dough, miss his presence in the room, a presence that had filled your life? Was ascension joy dwindling—for you and for the disciples?

I remember the saying: The measure of our desire is the degree to which it will be fulfilled. Did you powerfully intercede and hunger for his coming? Did you expect something to happen simply because it was a festival day? I read that it was sometime before nine o'clock in the morning when things began to happen (cf. Acts 2:15): "And suddenly from heaven there came a sound like the rush of a violent wind, and it filled the entire house where they were sitting. Divided tongues, as of fire, appeared among them, and a tongue rested on each of them. All of them were filled with the Holy Spirit and began to speak in other languages, as the Spirit gave them ability" (Acts 2:2–4).

And, Mary, did you know? Was it like that wonderful overshadowing some thirty-three years before? Was his presence in the room again—in the wind and flame, cloud and light, blessing hands and hovering dove, the water, the anointing, and the seal—never, ever to leave his people again?

Look out from the upper room with me, Mary, and see the dancing hearts of the new three thousand (cf. Acts 2:4). Take me with you to "the apostles' teaching and fellowship, to the breaking of bread and the prayers" (Acts 2:42).

THE ASSUMPTION

> In the ascension, Christ was raised in glory to the right
> hand of the Father, while Mary herself would be raised
> to that same glory in the assumption, enjoying before-
> hand, by a unique privilege, the destiny reserved for all
> the just at the resurrection of the dead (*On the Most
> Holy Rosary,* n. 23).

Mary, mother and sister to me, I looked for the origin
of the word "assumption," and found the Latin
assumere, "to take to oneself." I put aside all my schol-
arly books and fears to think about *assumere* and Jesus.
Now everything makes sense. Of course! Could it be
any other way? He who fashioned you, beautiful and all-
holy, made you a new creature formed in grace and favored, gave you the capacity for covenant realities like
no other—could he watch your body dissolve to dust?
You were his first home on earth—Word enfleshed in
you—and how he loved the things of earth you opened
wide for him! Now he takes you home to himself, fully.

You yourself are of the earth, but whole and unbro-
ken. You kept the covenant like no other. From the beginning to the end and beyond, you were with him.
Shall the grave consume your God-filled beauty? It

could, of course, as it will take my brokenness. But he took you to himself and lets you share his glory—God and creature, Father and child, Son and mother, Holy Spirit and overshadowed favored one—model for me of faith that believes in this eternal destiny and lives a life of love based on that belief. You become companion for me—and everyone—on the journey. And he chose to make it so!

I can search in vain in the holy books, Mary, to find the story of your last days. It's not there. I only know you went with John, but where and how is hassled over still. Jerusalem? Ephesus? I'd love to know, but surely it doesn't matter, for the ancients swear you are not at either place. You are home with him!

And isn't it said: As the Church prays, so she believes? From of old—as early as the second century—you were called the New Eve, the one who undid what our first mother had done. Eve is free. How she must be thankful that she is vindicated, and rejoice in her daughter! Liturgies and poetry, hymns and prayers, memorials of stone and heart-warming celebrations—all of these celebrate you not as a memory faded, but as living in eternal light, body and soul like Jesus is in his humanity, in heaven with him.

As I hold the cross of my beads, I remember the promise Jesus made to all of us baptized into him, and I believe him. I believe in the resurrection of the body and life everlasting. It is this teaching that tells me there is a purpose, a reason, and a brief season for all things now, but tomorrow there is a destiny most wonderful for each of us, if we but choose it. And I believe it, since it happened to you as he said. Why, Mary? Why is it important for me to know this? Is it to honor him all the more, for in you he shows me that he keeps his promise? When I begin to be afraid that my life lacks meaning, I look to you whose love is consummated in glory—the kingdom here and the kingdom to come. Your life teaches me that I and each of us are meant for love now and forever.

The beads slip by and I ask you again and again to pray for me at my dying. Will he come for me as he did for you? Will he present me to the Father, face to face, and will you be there? Will the Spirit purify the fire in my soul into a love transformed to resemble you, full of grace? Will it be the same for all those for whom I pray? This is my hope.

> In the most holy Virgin the Church has already reached that perfection whereby she exists without spot or wrinkle (*Lumen Gentium*, n. 65).

> In the bodily and spiritual glory which she possesses in heaven, the Mother of Jesus continues in this present world as the image and first flowering of the Church as it is to be perfected in the world to come. Likewise Mary shines forth until the day the Lord shall come (2 Pt 3:10) as a sign of sure hope and comfort for the pilgrim People of God (*Lumen Gentium*, n. 68).

Mary is crowned queen of heaven and earth

THE CORONATION

Crowned in glory—as she appears in the last glorious mystery—Mary shines forth as Queen of the Angels and Saints, the anticipation and the supreme realization of the eschatological state of the Church (*On the Most Holy Rosary,* n. 23).

"And now, you will conceive in your womb and bear a son, and you will name him Jesus. He will be great, and will be called the Son of the Most High, and the Lord God will give to him the throne of his ancestor David. He will reign over the house of Jacob for ever, and of his kingdom there will be no end" (Lk 1:31-33).

As mother of a king, Mary is a *Gebirah,* the queen mother, of Israel.[9] She shares the king's dignity, and has her place near him. He will hear her in questions great and small, for—sheltered in her womb, held in her arms, nursed at her breast—she is the place where his human heart first experienced love.

---

9. For more information on the queen mother, see: www.udayton.edu/mary/questions/yq2/yq282.html.

Lovers share their laurels, and they love to place rings on fingers and jewels everywhere, showering upon one another every type of gift. As God's Son, Jesus is a king, but also our redeemer, the new Adam. Mary may stand at his side, associated with him in everything as the new Eve. He loves her for it and will reward her faithfulness. This role of Mary is explained in *Ad Cæli Regina,* written by Pope Pius XII (October 11, 1954). In some nations at that time, the individual had no rights, no personal dignity, because of certain ideologies that wanted to crush Christianity. The pope turned to Mary to show the world the heights of human nobility achieved by those who live the Gospel of Christ and follow his example of service.

Through an excuse to obtain power and knowledge, Adam and Eve destroyed their realm. They refused to serve God's wish. Christ alone restores that kingdom of self-oblation and kingly service. He offers it back to us in the grace of Baptism. Mary, too, is called to serve. She is favored, graced. The word the angel addressed to her is found nowhere else in the Gospel, *kecharitòmenè,* the object of God's grace and favor, chosen for a long time past. In creating Mary, God restores full human dignity and nobility. As Jesus taught us, the highest expression of human sovereignty is the ability to serve, to lay down our lives for others. Mary uses this power to love God with all her heart and all her service. Her dignity is her unhesitating ready kindness to serve those in need—the ill, the oppressed, the poor. Down the centuries, the Church has never tired to call Mary queen and give her crowns, convinced that Jesus himself did so first. Coronation is the Church's grateful acknowledgement of Mary's readiness to serve.

> Since the Council of Ephesus, Mary is portrayed "as Queen and Empress seated upon a royal throne adorned with royal insignia, crowned with the royal diadem, and surrounded by the host of angels and saints in heaven, and ruling not only over nature and its powers, but also over the machinations of Satan. Iconography …has even taken the form of representing colorfully the divine Redeemer crowning his mother with a resplendent diadem *(Ad Cæli Regina,* n. 32).

Mary was called by the Father to be "a partner to Christ in the redemption of the human race" *(Ad Cæli Regina,* n. 38). Christ shares his power with her much like he promises it to his apostles, "But you will receive power when the Holy Spirit has come upon you; and you will be my witnesses…to the ends of the earth" (Acts 1:8). And what is that power? It is to know and use the dignity of queenly service. As the dwelling place of the Spirit since the beginning of her existence, Mary has been clothed with that power, with a dignity higher than all others. "From her union with Christ she receives the royal right to dispose of the treasures of the Divine Redeemer's Kingdom; from her union with Christ, finally, is derived the inexhaustible efficacy of her maternal intercession before the Son and his Father" (*Ad Cæli Regina*, n. 39).

Mary, it's time to celebrate, to shake off anxiety, and to prepare the festival. The King leads his queen mother to his throne! Our humanness is free and oh, so beautiful in you!

Children weave their wreaths, teens play at pageants, trademarks carry crowns, movies discover princesses, window banners call a people to rise up in dignity—everywhere, a proclamation of "the best." It was always so and shall not be taken away. Was your coronation one time and only then? We celebrate its continuation for we believe that you are among us, Mary, as we make our way on the journey. Just as we believe our Christ drew you to himself and crowned you in glory with tender love, so we also believe that he continues to send you to prepare his dwelling places among us—be this in spirit, in every Christian church, and even now and then in the flesh.

In times past, Aztecs joined the dance of millions to celebrate your coming as a little woman bearing Christ, with mercy and roses for a bishop. Some believe. Others will wait till the final day to test such beliefs of your presence among us. Nonetheless, it is

God who crowned you first and lets us join him in the dance of his love and praise.

And when we crown you, Mary, in the traditions of our cultures we use things of the earth—violets, roses, and filigree; gems, silver, and gold—to praise you, for you brought him to dance here with us for a time. And you crown us in return. We, too, share the throne and your nobility—love for love, crown for crown! That is our destiny. The dance whirls on and on—to thank you, to love him, and to look forward to the crown he has waiting for each one of us.

EPILOGUE

After speaking of the Church, her origin, mission, and destiny, we can find no better way to conclude than by looking to Mary. In her we contemplate what the Church already is in her mystery on her own "pilgrimage of faith," and what she will be in the homeland at the end of her journey. There, "in the glory of the Most Holy and Undivided Trinity," "in the communion of all the saints," the Church is awaited by the one she venerates as Mother of her Lord and as her own mother (CCC, n. 972).

Pope John Paul II's
Suggestions for the Rosary

The Four Sets of Rosary Mysteries

In his letter *On the Most Holy Rosary (Rosarium Virginis Mariæ)*, Pope John Paul II offered suggestions for praying the Rosary more fruitfully. He introduced a new set of mysteries, the mysteries of light or luminous mysteries, which focus on important events from the public life of Jesus. Formerly, the rosary bypassed Jesus' public ministry by going directly from his childhood to his passion. While any set of mysteries can be recited at any time, the Pope recommends the following pattern:

Joyful Mysteries: Mondays and Saturdays
Sorrowful Mysteries: Tuesdays and Fridays
Mysteries of Light: Thursdays
Glorious Mysteries: Wednesdays and Sundays

This indication is not intended to limit a rightful freedom in personal and community prayer, where account needs to be taken of spiritual and pastoral needs and of the occurrence of particular liturgical celebrations which might call for suitable adaptations. What is really important is that the Rosary should always be seen and experienced as a path of contemplation. In the Rosary, in a way similar to what takes place in the Liturgy, the Christian week, centered on Sunday, the day of resurrection, becomes a journey through the mysteries of the life of Christ, and he is revealed in the lives of his disciples as the Lord of time and of history (*On the Most Holy Rosary,* n. 38).

ADDITIONAL PRACTICES

Use an Icon to Set the Scene of Each Mystery

John Paul suggests using icons as a means of deepening one's meditation on the mysteries.

> Announcing each mystery, and perhaps even using a suitable icon to portray it, is as it were *to open up a scenario* on which to focus our attention. The words direct the imagination and the mind toward a particular episode or moment in the life of Christ. In the Church's traditional spirituality, the veneration of icons and the many devotions appealing to the senses, as well as the method of prayer proposed by Saint Ignatius of Loyola in the Spiritual Exercises, make use of visual and imaginative elements (the *compositio loci*), judged to be of great help in concentrating the mind on the particular mystery. This is a methodology, moreover, which *corresponds to the inner logic of the Incarnation:* in Jesus, God wanted to take on human features. It is through his

bodily reality that we are led into contact with the mystery of his divinity (*On the Most Holy Rosary,* n. 29).

Use of "Rejoice, Mary"

For the joyful mysteries, local cultural areas use *Rejoice, Mary* for the initial greeting.

Scripture scholars agree with Pope John Paul II that the Greek word *chaire* in Sacred Scripture would be rendered more closely to the original with *rejoice* rather than *hail,* when translating the angel's greeting to Mary. A suggestion is to render the wording: *Rejoice, Mary, the Lord is with you!* (1996) There is a similar issue in the title used to greet Mary (*gratia plena*, or 'full of grace' in the Latin Vulgate—*kecharitomene,* or 'highly favored one' in the Greek).[10]

Insert the Scripture Related to the Mystery

After the name of Jesus in each Hail Mary, add an "insert" *(clausulæ)* usually taken from Scripture related to the mystery. For example: "…and blessed is the fruit of your womb, Jesus, who died for us on the cross." This custom is well known in German speaking countries.

Pope Paul VI drew attention, in his Apostolic Exhortation *Marialis Cultus*, to the custom in certain regions of highlighting the name of Christ by the addition of a clause referring to the mystery being contemplated. This is a praiseworthy custom, especially during public

10. www.udayton.edu/mary/questions/yq/yq51.html

recitation. It gives forceful expression to our faith in Christ, directed to the different moments of the Redeemer's life. It is at once *a profession of faith* and an aid in concentrating our meditation, since it facilitates the process of assimilation to the mystery of Christ inherent in the repetition of the *Hail Mary* (*On the Most Holy Rosary,* n. 33).

Listen to the Word of God

After announcing the mystery, read a biblical passage that refers to it.

In order to supply a Biblical foundation and greater depth to our meditation, it is helpful to follow the announcement of the mystery with *the proclamation of a related Biblical passage,* long or short, depending on the circumstances. No other words can ever match the efficacy of the inspired word. As we listen, we are certain that this is the word of God, spoken for today and spoken "for me" (*On the Most Holy Rosary,* n. 30).

Be Aware of Silence

Listening and meditation are nourished by silence. After the announcement of the mystery and the proclamation of the word, it is fitting to pause and focus one's attention for a suitable period of time on the mystery concerned, before moving into vocal prayer. A discovery of the importance of silence is one of the secrets of practicing contemplation and meditation. One drawback of a society dominated by technology and the mass media is the fact that silence becomes increasingly difficult to achieve. Just as moments of silence are recommended in the Liturgy, so too in the recitation of the Rosary it is fitting to pause briefly after listening to the word of God, while the mind focuses on the content of a particular mystery (*On the Most Holy Rosary*, n. 31).

Prayer at the End of Each Decade

In current practice, the Trinitarian doxology is followed by a brief concluding prayer which varies according to local custom. Without in any way diminishing the value of such invocations, it is worthwhile to note that the contemplation of the mysteries could better express their full spiritual fruitfulness if an effort were made to conclude each mystery with *a prayer for the fruits specific to that particular mystery*. In this way the Rosary would better express its connection with the Christian life. One fine liturgical prayer suggests as much, inviting us to pray that, by meditation on the mysteries of the Rosary, we may come to "imitate what they contain and obtain what they promise" (taken from the Mass for the Feast of the Rosary) (*On the Most Holy Rosary*, n. 35).

POPE JOHN PAUL'S REFLECTIONS ON VARIOUS ELEMENTS OF THE ROSARY

The Beads

The traditional aid used for the recitation of the Rosary is the set of beads. At the most superficial level, the beads often become a simple counting mechanism to mark the succession of *Hail Marys*. Yet they can also take on a symbolism which can give added depth to contemplation.

Here the first thing to note is the way the beads converge upon the crucifix, which both opens and closes the unfolding sequence of prayer. The life and prayer of believers is centered upon Christ. Everything begins from him, everything leads toward him, everything, through him, in the Holy Spirit, attains to the Father....

A fine way to expand the symbolism of the beads is to let them remind us of our many relationships, of the bond of communion and fraternity which unites us all in Christ *(On the Most Holy Rosary,* n. 36).

The Our Father

After listening to the word and focusing on the mystery, it is natural for *the mind to be lifted up toward the Father*. In each of his mysteries, Jesus always leads us to the Father, for as he rests in the Father's bosom (cf. Jn 1:18) he is continually turned toward him. He wants us to share in his intimacy with the Father, so that we can say with him: "Abba, Father" (Rom 8:15; Gal 4:6). By virtue of his relationship to the Father he makes us brothers and sisters of himself and of one another, communicating to us the Spirit which is both his and the Father's. Acting as a kind of foundation for the Christological and Marian meditation which unfolds in the repetition of the *Hail Mary*, the *Our Father* makes meditation upon the mystery, even when carried out in solitude, an ecclesial experience *(On the Most Holy Rosary,* n. 32).

The Hail Mary (Rejoice, Mary)

This is the most substantial element in the Rosary and also the one which makes it a Marian prayer *par excellence.* Yet when the *Hail Mary* is properly understood, we come to see clearly that its Marian character is not opposed to its Christological character, but that it actually emphasizes and increases it. The first part of the *Hail Mary,* drawn from the words spoken to Mary by the Angel Gabriel and by Saint Elizabeth, is a contemplation in adoration of the mystery accomplished in the Virgin of Nazareth. These words express, so to speak, the wonder of heaven and earth; they could be said to give us a glimpse of God's own wonderment as he contemplates his "masterpiece"—the Incarnation of the Son in the womb of the Virgin Mary.... The repetition of the *Hail Mary* in the Rosary gives us a share in God's own wonder and pleasure: in jubilant amazement we acknowledge the greatest miracle of history. Mary's prophecy here finds its fulfillment: "Henceforth all generations will call me blessed" (Lk 1:48) (*On the Most Holy Rosary,* n. 33).

The Glory

Trinitarian doxology is the goal of all Christian contemplation. For Christ is the way that leads us to the Father in the Spirit. If we travel this way to the end, we repeatedly encounter the mystery of the three divine Persons, to whom all praise, worship, and thanksgiving are due. It is important that the *Gloria, the high-point of contemplation,* be given due prominence in the Rosary. In public recitation it could be sung, as a way of giving proper emphasis to the essentially Trinitarian structure of all Christian prayer.

To the extent that meditation on the mystery is attentive and profound, and to the extent that it is enlivened—from one Hail Mary to another—by love for Christ and for Mary, the glorification of the Trinity at the end of each decade, far from being a perfunctory conclusion, takes on its proper contemplative tone, raising the mind as it were to the heights of heaven and enabling us in some way to relive the experience of Tabor, a foretaste of the contemplation yet to come: "It is good for us to be here!" (Lk 9:33) *(On the Most Holy Rosary,* n. 34).

Repetition as a Dynamic of Love

Meditation on the mysteries of Christ is proposed in the Rosary by means of a method designed to assist in their assimilation. It is a method *based on repetition.* This applies above all to the *Hail Mary,* repeated ten times in each mystery. If this repetition is considered superficially, there could be a temptation to see the Rosary as a dry and boring exercise. It is quite another thing, however, when the Rosary is thought of as an outpouring of that love which tirelessly returns to the person loved with expressions similar in their content but ever fresh in terms of the feeling pervading them....To understand the Rosary, one has to enter into the psychological dynamic proper to love *(On the Most Holy Rosary,* n. 26).

ROSARY BASICS

HOW TO PRAY THE ROSARY

The Rosary is a Gospel prayer that helps us to pray with Mary so as to grow closer to her Son, Jesus. The heart of the Rosary is meditation on the mysteries of Jesus' life. We begin the Rosary by blessing ourselves with the crucifix and praying the Apostles' Creed, one Our Father, three Hail Marys and one Glory to the Father on the small chain. Then we pray one Our Father, ten Hail Marys and one Glory to the Father. This completes one decade, and the other decades are recited in the same manner, while meditating on the mystery for each decade. At the end of the Rosary, the Hail, Holy Queen and the Litany of the Blessed Virgin may be recited. The Memorare or prayers for the Holy Father are other options.

While this is the basic structure, Pope Paul VI, Pope John Paul II, and the American bishops have said that the Rosary can be modified to suit customs of local areas, spiritualities of Church movements, and personal preferences.

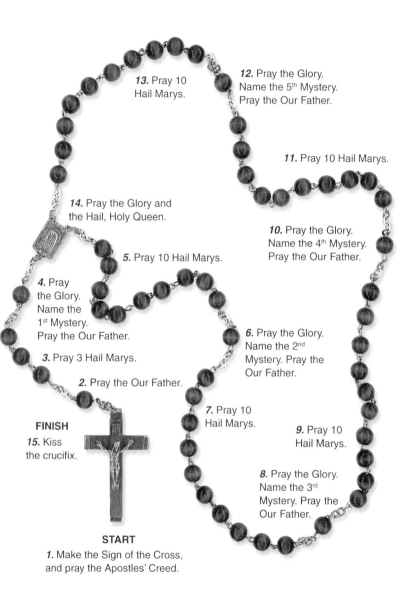

13. Pray 10 Hail Marys.

12. Pray the Glory. Name the 5th Mystery. Pray the Our Father.

11. Pray 10 Hail Marys.

14. Pray the Glory and the Hail, Holy Queen.

10. Pray the Glory. Name the 4th Mystery. Pray the Our Father.

5. Pray 10 Hail Marys.

4. Pray the Glory. Name the 1st Mystery. Pray the Our Father.

6. Pray the Glory. Name the 2nd Mystery. Pray the Our Father.

3. Pray 3 Hail Marys.

2. Pray the Our Father.

7. Pray 10 Hail Marys.

9. Pray 10 Hail Marys.

FINISH

15. Kiss the crucifix.

8. Pray the Glory. Name the 3rd Mystery. Pray the Our Father.

START

1. Make the Sign of the Cross, and pray the Apostles' Creed.

The Apostles' Creed

I believe in God, the Father almighty, creator of heaven and earth. I believe in Jesus Christ, his only Son, our Lord. He was conceived by the power of the Holy Spirit and born of the Virgin Mary. He suffered under Pontius Pilate, was crucified, died and was buried. He descended to the dead. On the third day he arose again. He ascended into heaven, and is seated at the right hand of the Father. He will come again to judge the living and the dead. I believe in the Holy Spirit, the holy Catholic Church, the communion of saints, the forgiveness of sins, the resurrection of the body, and life everlasting. Amen.

The Lord's Prayer

Our Father, who art in heaven, hallowed be thy name; thy kingdom come; thy will be done on earth as it is in heaven. Give us this day our daily bread, and forgive us our trespasses, as we forgive those who trespass against us, and lead us not into temptation, but deliver us from evil. Amen.

Hail Mary

Hail, Mary, full of grace! The Lord is with you. Blessed are you among women, and blessed is the fruit of your womb, Jesus. Holy Mary, Mother of God, pray for us sinners, now and at the hour of our death. Amen.

Glory

Glory to the Father, and to the Son, and to the Holy Spirit. As it was in the beginning, is now, and will be forever. Amen.

Hail, Holy Queen

Hail, holy Queen, Mother of mercy, our life, our sweetness, and our hope! To you we cry, poor banished children of Eve; to you we send up our sighs, mourning and weeping in this valley of tears. Turn then, most gracious advocate, your eyes of mercy toward us, and after this our exile, show unto us the blessed fruit of your womb, Jesus. O clement, O loving, O sweet Virgin Mary.

R. Pray for us, O Holy Mother of God.
V. *That we may be made worthy of the promises of Christ.*

Prayer to Conclude the Rosary

O God, whose only-begotten Son, by his life, death, and resurrection has purchased for us the rewards of eternal life, grant, we beseech you, that, meditating on these mysteries of the most holy Rosary of the Blessed Virgin Mary, we may imitate what they contain and obtain what they promise. Through the same Christ our Lord. Amen.

Memorare

Remember, O most gracious Virgin Mary, that never was it known that anyone who fled to your protection, implored your help or sought your intercession was left unaided. Inspired with this confidence, I fly to you, O Virgin of virgins, my Mother; to you I come; before you I kneel, sinful and sorrowful. O Mother of the Word Incarnate, despise not my petitions, but in your mercy hear and answer them. Amen.

Sub Tuum (We fly to your patronage)

We fly to your patronage, O holy Mother of God; despise not our petitions in our necessities, but deliver us always from all dangers, O glorious and blessed Virgin. *(Third century)*

Little Consecration

My Queen, My Mother, I give myself entirely to you, and to show my devotion to you I consecrate to you this day my eyes, my ears, my mouth, my heart, my entire self without reserve. As I am your own, my good Mother, guard me and defend me as your property and possession. Amen.

(Seventeenth century)

To Mary of the Annunciation

May all generations proclaim you blessed, O Mary. You believed the Archangel Gabriel, and in you were fulfilled all the great things that the angel had announced to you. With my entire being I praise you, O Mary. You had faith in the Incarnation of the Son of God in your virginal womb, and you became the Mother of God. When you said "yes," the Eternal Word became man and lived among us. Then the happiest day in the history of the human race dawned. Humanity received the Divine Master, the Good Shepherd, Jesus, the Way, Truth and Life.

Blessed be the Lord, who willed to give us everything through you. Faith is a gift of God and the root of every good. O Mary, obtain for us a lively, firm and active faith. May we treasure the words of your blessed Son, as you preserved them in your heart and prayerfully pondered them. May the Gospel be brought to everyone, with every means available. May all people receive it so that they may become, in Jesus Christ, children of God (cf. Jn 1:12). Amen. *(Blessed James Alberione)*

The Litany of the Blessed Virgin

Lord, *have mercy on us.*
Christ, *have mercy on us.*
Lord, *have mercy on us.*

Christ, *hear us.*
Christ, *graciously hear us.*

God the Father of heaven, *have mercy on us.*
God the Son, Redeemer of the world,
    have mercy on us.
Holy Trinity, one God, *have mercy on us.*

Holy Mary, *pray for us.*
Holy Mother of God, *pray for us.*
Holy Virgin of virgins, *pray for us.*
Mother of Christ, *pray for us.*
Mother of the Church, *pray for us.*
Mother of divine grace, *pray for us.*
Mother most pure, *pray for us.*
Mother most chaste, *pray for us.*

Mother inviolate, *pray for us.*
Mother undefiled, *pray for us.*
Mother most amiable, *pray for us.*
Mother most admirable, *pray for us.*
Mother of good counsel, *pray for us.*
Mother of our Creator, *pray for us.*
Mother of our Redeemer, *pray for us.*
Virgin most prudent, *pray for us.*
Virgin most venerable, *pray for us.*
Virgin most renowned, *pray for us.*
Virgin most merciful, *pray for us.*
Virgin most faithful, *pray for us.*
Mirror of justice, *pray for us.*
Seat of wisdom, *pray for us.*
Cause of our joy, *pray for us.*
Vessel of honor, *pray for us.*
Singular vessel of devotion, *pray for us.*
Mystical rose, *pray for us.*
Tower of David, *pray for us.*
Tower of ivory, *pray for us.*
House of gold, *pray for us.*
Ark of the covenant, *pray for us.*
Gate of heaven, *pray for us.*
Morning star, *pray for us.*
Health of the sick, *pray for us.*
Refuge of sinners, *pray for us.*

Comforter of the afflicted, *pray for us.*
Help of Christians, *pray for us.*
Queen of angels, *pray for us.*
Queen of patriarchs, *pray for us.*
Queen of prophets, *pray for us.*
Queen of apostles, *pray for us.*
Queen of martyrs, *pray for us.*
Queen of confessors, *pray for us.*
Queen of virgins, *pray for us.*
Queen of all saints, *pray for us.*
Queen conceived without original sin,
    pray for us.
Queen assumed into heaven, *pray for us.*
Queen of the most holy rosary, *pray for us.*
Queen of peace, *pray for us.*
Queen of families, *pray for us.*

Lamb of God, you take away the sins of the
    world, *spare us, O Lord.*
Lamb of God, you take away the sins of the
    world, *graciously hear us, O Lord.*
Lamb of God, you take away the sins of the
    world, *have mercy on us.*

R. Pray for us, O holy Mother of God.
V. *That we may be made worthy of the prom-
    ises of Christ.*

Let us pray.

O God, whose only-begotten Son by his life, death and resurrection has purchased for us the rewards of eternal salvation, grant, we pray, that meditating upon these mysteries in the most holy rosary of the Blessed Virgin Mary, we may imitate what they contain and obtain what they promise. Through Christ our Lord. Amen.

THE ROSARY'S HISTORY

The Rosary prayer as we know it today was established and standardized as an approved prayer of the Church by Pope St. Pius V in 1569. By 1573, this same pope set down the liturgical feast of the Rosary, and by 1716, this feast was extended to the whole Church. It is celebrated as a memorial on October 7.

Through the centuries there have been many church documents on the Rosary. For example, Pope Leo XIII (1878–1903) wrote thirteen encyclicals on the Rosary. Each pope since then has written something on the Rosary. Pope John Paul II wrote an Apostolic Letter on the Rosary *(Rosarium Virginis Mariæ)* in which he proclaimed October 2002 to October 2003, "The Year of the Rosary" *(RVM* 3). In his letter, Pope John Paul II established a new set of Rosary mysteries, the luminous mysteries, which include the public life of the Lord.

The Church has granted rich and varied privileges to the Rosary. In the document *Marialis Cultus,* Pope Paul VI recommended that the Rosary be prayed before or after Mass, *but not during Mass.* That there is a Rosary prayer devotion and a liturgy of the Church celebrating the power of that prayer indicates the intimate link between the two and a recommended public place of praying the Rosary.

The Rosary is frequently prayed during adoration hours before the Blessed Sacrament, at shrines, on pilgrimages, and privately, for instance at one's own home shrine.

For more detailed information on the origin of the Rosary prayer and Rosary beads see the Mary Page on the website of The Marian Library/International Marian Research Institute, an international center of research and study on the role of Mary in Christian life.

An index of Rosary topics and reflections can be found at: www.udayton.edu/mary/resources/rosdex. html

M. Jean Frisk, S.T.L. is a member of the secular institute of the Schoenstatt Sisters of Mary (ISSM). She holds a licentiate in sacred theology from The Marian Library/International Marian Research Institute in Dayton, Ohio, where she helps publish the Mary Page (www.udayton.edu/Mary). Her area of study is Mary in catechesis. She is an instructor and consultant regarding Marian teachings and wrote the introductions to the Church documents on Mary in the collection *Mother of Christ, Mother of the Church* (Pauline Books & Media). Although often "on the road regarding things Marian," Sister Jean resides at the International Schoenstatt Center in Waukesha, Wisconsin, where she writes "in the shadow of Mary's shrine."

Pauline
BOOKS & MEDIA

The Daughters of St. Paul operate book and media centers at the following addresses. Visit, call or write the one nearest you today, or find us on the World Wide Web, www.pauline.org

CALIFORNIA

3908 Sepulveda Blvd, Culver City, CA 90230   310-397-8676

5945 Balboa Avenue, San Diego, CA 92111   858-565-9181

46 Geary Street, San Francisco, CA 94108   415-781-5180

FLORIDA

145 SW 107th Avenue, Miami, FL 33174   305-559-6715

HAWAII

1143 Bishop Street, Honolulu, HI 96813   808-521-2731

Neighbor Islands call: 800-259-8463

ILLINOIS

172 North Michigan Avenue, Chicago, IL 60601
312-346-4228

LOUISIANA

4403 Veterans Memorial Blvd, Metairie, LA 70006   504-887-7631

MASSACHUSETTS

885 Providence Hwy, Dedham, MA 02026   781-326-5385

MISSOURI

9804 Watson Road, St. Louis, MO 63126   314-965-3512

NEW JERSEY

561 U.S. Route 1, Wick Plaza, Edison, NJ 08817   732-572-1200

NEW YORK

150 East 52nd Street, New York, NY 10022   212-754-1110

78 Fort Place, Staten Island, NY 10301   718-447-5071

PENNSYLVANIA

9171-A Roosevelt Blvd, Philadelphia, PA 19114   215-676-9494

SOUTH CAROLINA

243 King Street, Charleston, SC 29401   843-577-0175

TENNESSEE

4811 Poplar Avenue, Memphis, TN 38117   901-761-2987

TEXAS

114 Main Plaza, San Antonio, TX 78205   210-224-8101

VIRGINIA

1025 King Street, Alexandria, VA 22314   703-549-3806

CANADA

3022 Dufferin Street, Toronto, Ontario, Canada M6B 3T5   416-781-9131

1155 Yonge Street, Toronto, Ontario, Canada M4T 1W2   416-934-3440

¡También somos su fuente para libros, videos y música en español!